AF230075

Taste of Change

Poems

Wesley D. Sims

Iris Press Chapbook Series
Oak Ridge, Tennessee

Copyright © 2019 by Wesley D. Sims

All rights reserved. No portion of this book may be reproduced in any form or by any means, including electronic storage and retrieval systems, without explicit, prior written permission of the author, except for brief passages excerpted for review and critical purposes.

ISBN: 978-1-60454-508-1

Cover Photo: "Meadow in Blairsville, GA" by Alfred Schrock
www.puregeorgiaphotography.com

Author Photo: LifeTouch Photography
www.lifetouch.com

Book Design: Robert B. Cumming, Jr.

Iris Publishing Group, Inc
www.irisbooks.com

Acknowledgments

Thanks to the editors of following publications in which the following poems first appeared in some form.

American Diversity Report: "Identity Theft" and "Taste of Change"
Amore: Love Poems Anthology: "Second Journey"
CT Review: "Lucky Strikes"
The Avocet Journal: "Ode to a Sweet Gum Tree," "Snake Battle," and "Bag Limit"
The Weekly Avocet: "Letter to the Ocean," "Winter Cavern Out My Window," and "Spring in Haiku"
Chattanooga Writer's Guild 2017 Anthology: "Metaphors"
The Grace of God Anthology: "Wings"
The Griffin: "Sleep Child"
Liquid Imagination: "Ordinary Heroes"
Magnets and Ladders: "Clinical Diagnosis"
Migrants and Stowaways, an Anthology of Journeys: "If I Go Suddenly"
Nature Writing: "Ode to a Mallard" and "Praise for a Swallow's Nest"
On the Veranda: "Copperhead"
SLANT: "Divining Rod"
The Tennessee Magazine: "January in the Smokies" and "Sunset at Fooshee Pass"
Wisconsin Review: "Reluctant Feet"

Thanks to my friends in the Chattanooga Poetry Critique Group, in Connie Green's Chapbook Class, and in the Poetry Pie Group, many of whom have listened attentively to some of these poems and some of whom have provided feedback.

Contents

To Barbara, Melody, Joy, Daryl, Nathan, Daniel

We faced change together,
through good times and bad, with laughter and tears,
sometimes with sorrow, sometimes rejoicing,
but through it all kept the faith and persevered.

Nature

January in the Smokies

Gone is the fog-scumbled green cover
of summer mornings and the kaleidoscope
of October color in the Smokies.
January snow has saddled limbs of hickory
and maple and fir, assaulted with bullets of ice,
chased the sun into its solar house above the atmosphere.

Early twilight paints the scenery black and white.
The moon, a pale gold ghost, peers out
at midnight through its gray parka of clouds.
Bunches of underbrush become interlinked igloos,
making Eskimos of sheltering birds and rabbits.
Shivering deciduous trees raise their frozen fingers
heavenward, praying in unison for winter's end.

Winter Cavern Out My Window

Yesterday snow slipped in, ghosted
my world a glorious white, brought
a respite from winter doldrums. But
late day warming brought sorrow
of melting, water glistening on
diminishing whiteness. This morning
I loitered at breakfast savoring my
tea and jelly toast. Opening the
curtains I beheld another wonder-
land. The melt on my roof had
built huge icicles, stalactites
of ice hanging from my gutter.
Drizzle of water down the sides
dazzled in sunlight. I thought
how even demise and decay
can disguise miracles.
Just like dying summer
stages the circus of
autumn leaves, so in
the gray and white
palette of winter,
miracles often
occur, there for
the observant
eye, the alert
and grate-
ful
I.

Ordinary Heroes

Dawn yawned the day half-awake.
Cardinals jostled the morning,
circled the sunflower feeder.
The sun pulled itself from treetops
limb to limb. It glared
at a murder of crows
flocking to the aid of a brother
disputing with the blue jays.
The sky grimaced, a swarm
of clouds from the north
plotted to hide the sun,
bring back the night.
The west wind whined.

A pair of common house sparrows
proclaimed their trust in the future,
chirped their mutual admiration.
She fluttered feathery charms,
he responded with breakfast,
served one grain at a time.
They sealed their promises with kisses
of millet and maize.
The wind sighed a hymn of gratitude
and pushed the clouds back
over the horizon. The sun beamed
like a proud parent. Mother
of morning smiled
and allowed Day to continue.

Ode to a Sweet Gum Tree

A fixture beside the campground lake,
you watched the children play,
cooled their brow with gentle breeze,
shaded adults seeking respite from the sun.
Your nightly scheduled concerts
serenaded us with crickets and tree frogs.
Your summer shawl of green
beckoned bluebirds and titmice
to your branches, offered home sites
for squirrels and crows.

Now like any self respecting lady
you've had a wardrobe change for Fall.
Not to imitate your neighbor dogwoods
who sport their brilliant crimson,
you've draped your shoulders
with deep purple, patterned
with five pointed stars,
like a little slice of evening sky.
Be discreet now,
don't gossip with the harvest moon
about the nighttime talk you've heard,
the quarrels of weary spouses,
the secret whispers of star-struck lovers.

Copperhead

Remember how we jaunted one sunny Spring
morning through the back pasture
carelessly parting johnson grass and joe-pye weed,
headed to a work session at the church cemetery?
Where we paused to climb through the fence
at the dirt road, a copperhead kept silent vigil,
spotted string of brown and copper
like a sisal rope pushed into an "S,"
sampling heat with a devilish tongue,
ready to spring against intruders.

You cringed, breathless, screamed and pointed.
Luck brought a neighbor on the same journey
along the road just in time.
A quick strike of his
hoe clipped its head and we tiptoed
on along the tree-lined road to the church,
scanning ditches and fence rows like mine sweepers.
We chopped crabgrass and dandelions around dead relatives
for hours, peering behind every dusty tombstone,
expecting some demonic clump of weeds to grow
copper spots, lunge and bruise our heels.

Sunset at Fooshee Pass Cove

Late day sky above the cove
has morphed from pale cerulean
into sapphire and shades of gray.
Ridges of hardwoods and pine
accent the mural with summer green.

Clouds coagulate around retreating sun.
The sun sector of sky blooms
yellowish-gold, then rose.
A massive swath of sky flames
into reddish-orange in a slow motion
slideshow, gleams like a giant gemstone.
The lake shimmers, then stills to a mirror
reflecting a big blanket of orange.

The cove yawns, its eyelids
slowly droop down on the sky.
The woods retreat inside their house
of darkness and close the door on day.

Letter to the Ocean

From a distance you appear placid
as a sunbather, on a vast, sky-canopied bed.
Closer, I find you a restless leviathan,
alive with repetitive motion.
You recede, surge, crash on the beach,
foam, swirl, dissolve into sand.

Your distant murmuring drew me,
undecipherable language from the deep.
Up close your roaring thunders above all
sounds. Stew of sea creatures and algae
awakens my senses. Brine-washed air bathes
my skin. Your color shifts like a cuttle fish,
blue to green to dappled gray and white,
the color of a fog-veiled morning sky
speckled with current-surfing sea gulls.

Seaside, I contemplate your fluid
movements, your wriggling waves, swelling
and waning, dancing for the moon;
and your cyclic washing and crashing.
I sense beneath the roar, a symphony playing—
flutes of wind, trumpets of gulls and terns,
drumbeat of breakers, bass blasts of boat horns.
My weary body hears the music,
feels the rhythm of the universe.

My cells seem to connect, like salt water to
salt water, as though I've always known you.
As though I should lie down beside you when
all my molecules return to water and earth.

Spring in Haiku

Yellow daffodils
scout and skirmish with winter,
probe the cold landscape.

Pansies and crocus
brave the frosty earth to fly
their bright, bold colors.

Hyacinths raise masts,
array their band of trumpets,
blare purple and pink.

Saucer magnolias
unveil new buds of promise,
candle tips glow white.

Ode to a Mallard

You waddle through green grass
to the campsite next door, regular client
at your noisily-guarded snack station,
solicit handouts with polite requests,
but your sleek body, adorned
with mottled brown, white, and blue
feathers, reveals no poverty of food.
Tossed morsels downed, you strut
back to the lake and mount
the shimmering green water
like a king ascending his throne.

You skim the placid surface,
pull a gentle wake behind, churn
of foot-paddles disguised underneath.
Green-crowned head gleams in sunlight.
Nearby drakes quack their complaints,
can't hide their jealousy, tinged
with envy as you glide along,
head erect, a belly full of special
rations and a striking new female
in tow, her glistening body
white as fluffy clouds, graceful
as a long-necked swan.

Praise for a Swallow's Nest

Late afternoon, sun lolling
toward the line of cool respite,
I mount my boat, camera on my neck,
launch another camping summer,
hoping to find an osprey
slow to lift off her house of sticks
atop a navigation signpost in the lake,
or a great blue heron lingering
like a blue and gray statue on a limb.

I sweep a wide circle, sidle up
to a thin finger of peninsula
where I last snapped a flock of herons
perched in brown pine tops.
I throttle down and glide
the silvery surface toward the bank,
angle for a closer view
of a gray and white tree swallow.

And then as if steered by serendipity,
the boat drifts into branches
of a fallen sweet gum.
The leaf-screen opens, and six feet
from my face two baby swallows
stretch in their exposed nest,
blind, downy heads lifted high,
caverns of yellow-rimmed mouths
open wide in trust that I bring
food, another day's manna
delivered from the sky.

Tell Me, Heron

You wait in freeze-frame,
picture of patience, feet
affixed to the sweet gum limb
jutting over the lake. Does time
operate in different domains,
day and night and seasons
parsed differently for me than you?

At long intervals your elegant gray
head ratchets robot-like to scan the next
lake sector, searching flash of small fins,
your daily bread, life for life, the natural
laws you use without the need to
understand or judge.

Minutes later, stilt legs stalk a few
steps left and apparent periscopic
neck adjusts to sight down spear-
pointed beak at different angle.

When I close the distance between
us, you yield your space with
but a squawk, ascend on two stout
wing flaps, and cruise to the last
lookout limb at mouth of cove. I ignore
you for thirty minutes, continue
casting my bait.

Finished fishing your cove I make
ready to leave, then spot you perched
on that dead pine trunk, blue and silver
statue to simple living topping a totem pole.
Tell me, heron—is it just your ancient
gene bestowed or has living by the lake

honed your patience, boosted your trust
to live day to day with no hurry,
no storing up for tomorrow?

Snake Battle

A long king snake stalks a large copperhead,
racing close, seizes the copperhead's tail
to thwart escape. The copper curls
back, lunges, lands two bites.
Immune to the poison, the king snake ignores
the bites, a small cost for a sumptuous meal.
The two serpents parry and thrust,
thrash and slap the ground,
white spots on the king flash
like stars twinkling on a black strip of sky.

The king lassoes the viper near its midsection.
Like thick colorful lariats knotted together,
they roll and whipsaw end around end
until they tumble into the river.
Writhing and splashing like mating mud turtles,
they bob, flop and float downstream a few yards.
A desperate surge of energy,
the copper hooks a branch, hoists
himself onto land, still lugging
the black and white speckled burden.
The hungry king tightens his grasp,
maneuvers to clamp the copper's neck,
wriggles his body forward, coiling
his prey like a wound spring.

Primitive math, ancient as reptiles,
addition and subtraction, one creature survives
when another perishes.
The mottled copper limp, motionless,
the king unwinds its deadly coil,
repositions head to head, begins
to swallow the hot meal head first
like a very slow motion scene
of a heron gulping down a big fish.

Bag Limit

I hush the alarm at 5:00 AM,
sheath my body in warm camos,
sleuth across the quiet field,
frost covered pasture and sage grass,
like a mottled, moving tree.
Dawn begins to thaw light from darkness.
I linger at woods edge to scout
and praise the new, unspoiled day,
glimpse an eight point buck
nosing around under a massive
white oak some seventy yards downhill.
Its soft tan coat has thickened
for winter, yet a full moon away.
I creep closer and hide beside
a small bushy pine, wait for him to offer
a better view. The approaching sun
fires up my brain cells and I ponder
a poem teasing my mind these past days.
I conjure a couple of new images
and cycle through some verbs,
test and taste them, choose a few
robust enough to delight my soul,
as the morning deer delights
in his bountiful crop of acorns.
When he turns, I prop my
hiking stick against a maple
and make ready
my camera, content this day
to bag a poem and a picture.

Psalm of Green

Yea, though I trudge through
the mountains and the valleys
of illness, I will not fear,
for the God of nature journeys with me.
I am led to verdant fields.
Green comforts me like a friend.
Olive oil shall anoint my salads.
The stem, seed, and flower sustain me.
When hosts prepare a table for me,
in the presence of friends or enemies,
I shall rejoice and dine with gusto.
I will stroll often beside emerald waters.
Surely mercy shall accompany me,
and I will celebrate health, and prosper
in the land of superb colors—green,
and orange. Plus red, white, and blue—
forever.

People

Taste of Change

He learned to hate at an early age
everything green spooned onto his plate.
It repelled as if monsters
curled on the dish lying in wait
to inject their slimy poison.

It offended his taste,
turnip green aroma distorted his face
like green-persimmon pucker,
evoked words sharp as epithets
spewing from his mouth.

Tasting the bitter herbs of physical changes,
grieving the health of immortal youth
prompted walks in the park,
but old habits clung like twining ivy,
comfortable as well worn shoes.

Freedom came late in life,
learning to tolerate diversity of color,
to relish the good inside,
to love red, yellow, green,
to savor each healthy gift.

The impetus came unexpected,
unbidden as a raven at his door,
strong as the fire of a cloudless sunrise,
easy as a quick journey on the train of motivation,
the conductor a white-coated stranger

named Verdict—*Positive*, he said,
your biopsy tested positive.

Divining Rod

I envied my grandfather.
Forked peach tree limb gripped
upright between fingers and thumb,
he strode in measured gait
and watched for the branch
to sense the underground flow,
to turn downward
as if it owned muscle and bone.
One time, he told me, he explored
for water at Mr. Jackson's place,
searched one direction then another,
detected the convergence
of two strong streams
and stepped it off.
Twenty paces, he declared,
if they'd shifted the puny well
that far south, the liquid of life
would have pooled up to 30 feet
below the surface.

I tried the mysterious craft
once, when too young, too timid
with halfhearted commitment.
It stood motionless,
a dumb branch in my hands.
I wish I could transplant
perseverance now to then
and master that art.
I too could detect invisible streams.
Perhaps I could have felt
a tuned fork tug and twist
to find the spring of fluid
pooling in my father's lung,
before that dark well overflowed
and drowned so much.

Second Journey

Husband four years dead,
she had sworn off men,
a spiritless traveler
in from the shallows.

A new friend sailed into port,
cheerful sunshine to lift morning fog.
Her wildly rushing river of words
slowed to a gentle stream.
Where it settled calm and deep
they savored silence.

Attentive eyes sparked jewels
of light that danced about her eyes.
Daily smiles blanked years
of rock-strewn memories.
Worn and weary hands found energy,
grew eager as young lovers,
reached out to chart new waters.
She set her sail for a second journey,
unloaded doubts to embark again.
Mums flourished on the sunny shore,
their blooms friendly faces
cheering at dockside.

But before her mums
could grace three autumns,
cancer raised its bold black flag.
And death, that captain of surprises,
remapped her course
for a port too far.

Wings

On my grandchild's graduation

It seems just yesterday my fingers fluttered
to show you how the birds fly.
You toddled out beside me,
and we watched the bluebirds dart
from limb to limb, butterflies float
among the marigolds and zinnias.
But the years have zoomed away
like doves on the wing,
and we celebrate a milestone.
You'll smile the smile of youth
when I say, *You've grown too fast.*
Poised like a baby robin
at nest's edge, flexing downy muscles,
you're ready to sample the air of freedom.
I worried at times your shelter
did not span the needed reach.
But I must applaud your mom's amazing work
and keeping two hands at the task.

The words *Don't fly* hang in my throat.
But time will no more cease its passing
than trees in spring will reel their buds back.
And so I offer this advice.
Spread your newfound wings,
leap high and leave the common run
of earth below, ascend until you find
the paths where eagles soar.
Beware the tricky currents,
seek shelter when the storms rise
and map the lay of land
that you called home.
Set your compass with the one

who divided earth from sky.
And don't neglect to journey back
and let us honor the success you wear.
I'll swallow my words of limitation,
persuade my throat to utter *Bon voyage,*
and raise my hand
to calm a fluttering
heart.

Lucky Strikes

The macho emblem covered your heart,
red circle of the cigarette pack shining
through your shirt pocket. The youth
of my time sang their jingle. Now you carry
the circle inside, left lung, upper lobe.
But for age and complications,
your chest would boast a stenciled emblem,
target for an X-ray gun. You're not the first

we watched go down in smoke. Sister trained
two years before on a red-target husband.
They measured darkness with medicine,
desperate smokes, and holes in the carpet.

The last trip out you dragged your breath
behind, tube encircling your head like a python.
Now you puff the pipe of therapy and bronchial
dilators. Steroids are your new friends. The blood
pressure cuff coils beside your water glass like
a poised serpent. Chest heaving with every draft,
you skip breaths to cough the frothy poison.

I've watched you count lost time and ceiling
tiles at three a.m. Days stitched together with naps
in your chrome-barred prison, and with waiting—
for daylight, for breakfast, for nurses, for shift change,
for nighttime, for tomorrow, for the end of waiting.

You draw deep from the reservoir of your
trademark sense of humor to still quip
one-liners about a body that shuns control.
Gasps and groans punctuate your sleep,
begging both life and expiration. Perhaps

you could have quit had it not been
addictive, but only a pleasure choice, as the ads
claimed, recounting no-proof stories. But I count
parched throats that try to hack the dark spot out.

The ghosts of victims past might wish
a different brand of lucky strikes—
lightning bolts to light them all,
smoke curling to the stars to avenge
ashen souls with burnt holes in their bones.

Sleep, Child

I join the gentle flow of visitors down
the hall, find faces of resignation sprinkled
like fallen leaves settled on a stream,
floating downward, their destinies rivered
to resolution by storm or shoal or mercy
of night. Is time the intercessor
for the pallid faces peering nowhere?

Inanimate objects blur with the living.
You must look close, like scanning
a forest floor to see what moves.
Pillows hold and also hide. A pile of clothes
cuddles in a chair. Walkers prop against
thin statues garbed in loose gowns.

I find the one I call *Aunt* near the nurses'
station, slumped in a wheelchair,
a small doll clasped in her arms.
The face is hers, and the eyes, but
an undecipherable gaze pierces me.
I cannot tell if she knows me.

"See my baby," she greets. I try
to converse but must finish the sentences.
Her mouth spills fragments—"I told them…
but they…, but it doesn't… I need…."
Thoughts tumble through tangled ganglions,
get snipped and split apart like water
parted by rocks in a fall.

For a moment the river flows
backward. I see myself as a child,
her daughter beside me,
as we stand and gesture,
hold a finger skyward, and sing
This Little Light of Mine.

"Sleep, child," echoes down the hall.
I strain to focus, glimpse a faint rocking motion.
Sleep draws a tide of comfort.
I wonder which voice beckons the tide.

Clinical Diagnosis

Two week visit at the clinic,
plethora of tests, team of doctors.
Good afternoon, I'm Dr. A. We need more tests.

Forms, questions, surveys greet us like beggars
with their hands out—*Have you ever…?*
When did you last…? On a scale of one to ten…?

We feed bales of paperwork to the computer
like hay to an elephant one handful at a time.
Dr. B: *When we get results, we'll compile a report.*

Storm of tests and appointments ends,
brings relief like Spring after a long winter.
Good morning, we're reviewing your reports.

Last day, last appointment, lead doctor.
Good afternoon, I'm Dr. Z, we're not certain,
but think it may be only stress.

We ponder reports, doctors' comments,
tentative diagnosis, and conclude—you will live
for the rest of your uncertain life.

Appointments over, leaving the lobby,
I watch you go pale, quiet. Hail a taxi.
Get you to bed as another episode hits.

Awake, you whisper, *I want to go home.*
Hours drag, night crawls, tense ride home.
Life resumes, illness continues just as before.

Reluctant Feet

Willing before the nausea returned,
now they pushed me out the back door,
past flowers suffering neglect.
They led me to her garden plot,
stood me at the edge
facing West where rows
of sweet corn ought to be,
tomatoes and squash, good listeners
all, before her body declined
beyond the hope of words.

I lifted my head to glimpse
against the darkened sky three
crows in procession South
toward the oak tree whose dead
limb points a finger at the empty pond.
Black-suited judges cawed their dissent.

The clay earth softened beneath me.
My feet melded to it.
I bargained with them to take me
back, bribed them with a promise
hard to keep. They kicked a clump
of dirt to scatter on the fruitless sod.

They've always been good soldiers.
Could they somehow know
they cannot stay where the heart
is not committed? They plodded
back toward the dim light
of Sister's window,
along the path her steps had traced,
a path now hard to follow.

Metaphors

Thinks in metaphor—words spoken
of an accomplished writer. I'd covet
such praise, silver words to chisel on my
stone. I peruse the poems, their metaphors
vibrant, lucid and copious as tomatoes
on the vine I pampered and tried to clone.

I ponder them, drooling, late nights
in my study, gaze like bejeweled seer
at creases in a yielded palm, peer
through translucent curtains
to conjure a crystal ball in soft light,
a globe to hover and consult that I might
call up some miracle, make luminous
words come forth from one whose lips
point me to a cavern, where on dark walls
I can trace and analyze the glyphs
to decipher a metaphoric secret.

I've turned examples on their back, took
sharp elbows of jabbing consonants,
felt soft vowel syllables soar and rise
with lively slopes and curves along
the track that takes a turn to hook
a sad or humorous surprise.
I've rolled them 'round my tongue
like butterscotch drops, sweet action
hoping for at least sublingual benefaction.

But I struggle with it, mine seem slow
and awkward like steps of a saddle horse
trashing corn, a first attempt behind the plow.
The time is late now, and do I dance for rain
clouds after old cornstalks have bowed
in dry surrender? So I dream an easy fix,
conceived as by some midnight notion
of wild eyed-scientist, with hopeful brow
pouring his tube of foggy potion.
I stoop to wish a microscopic strand
of DNA stripped off, swirled in some solution
in a Petri dish, made ready for infusion—
of metaphor-making gene transplant.

Paces

August, season of dog days,
when life should laze, drift along
on the torpid train of summer.

She showed me how to ride it,
to pack up my thoughts
and cruise an unhurried journey.

She loved the slow rhythm
of savoring the present,
tuning in to nature, strolling
among marigolds and zinnias.

But I look back now,
perceive a different pace.

A ruby-throated hummingbird
swoops down to my feeder,
gray-green blur of wings,
to sip the blood-tinted sustenance.

On the deck a cardinal
searching manna tilts her head,
spreads wings and lifts off
before I can raise my hand.

In the yard a gray squirrel
skitters in staccato time
up the clouded Sycamore,
arcs out of sight,
like a soul ascending.

And I recall that stunning day,
Mother dropped in her chair,
her chin still against her chest,
no time to say goodbye.

Circle of Cousins

In memory of Cindy

Your blonde hair shone like moonglow
in the days of our youth, in the memory
I ponder—you and your teenaged
cousin-pal in a faded photo, all smiles
in green summer shorts and red tops.
She traveled south in summer,
younger brother in tow, and we four,
like amateur explorers, traipsed over
pastures and fields. We turned stones, reveled
in the teeming dirt, chased rat snakes
and frogs, June bugs and butterflies, floated
like fluffy clouds above us, dirty-faced
angels in a carefree world. A tight family
circle, love's best geometry, a perfect shape,
like the moon and stars that ban darkness.

Last time I saw you, nature had begun its
dress rehearsal for autumn's celebration.
But your pale, splotched cheeks no longer
mimicked tinted maple leaves. Your gray,
thinned hair and purple lips reflected shades
of winter. I felt the smile vanish like short
seasons of our youth as your words
conveyed resignation to the fate you knew
loomed hard ahead. But I said still we'd dance
again some future morning.

Your tongue had grown thick last time
we talked, when you spoke of pain, declared
morphine your new best friend.
I prayed you'd slip gently from that prison,
but waited too long to call again, forgetting
the insistent reaper stalks the weak like
a lean-ribbed wolf exploiting moonlight.

I wish a loving place for you now,
perhaps the hearth of your son.
I picture a blonde earthen urn to encircle
you, keep your transformed
atoms through the long, long
night, while your grandchildren
learn to remember your name.

Identity Theft

Not her
credit card snatched,
nor driver's license,
nor picture ID.
Not her universal number
intercepted on the Internet.
Not the checkbook swiped
while her head was turned,
nor bank account number
pilfered from a pile of trash.

Instead,
radiance snatched from her brow,
her voice knocked down an octave,
shoulders drooped from weight
of falling self-esteem.
Pride ripped from her psyche,
guilt smeared on her mirror,
ugliness glaring from the future
like a finger-wagging stepmother.
She sees *Used* scrawled across her forehead,
dreams the only wedding dresses
available are ones already worn.
She winces remembering his gaze,
shivers at the thought of solitude,
freezes at the prospect of another intimacy.

No person
near to abort
the theft, he forced her
into an alley, stripped
away her innocence, tore off
her self respect, ripped off
her smile, her confidence,
stole her special gift. Filled her
future with depression and fear.

Floods

No time for consulting Noah
that stormy day in mid-July.
Molecules congregated,
clouds unleashed their downpour.

Shoal Creek rampaged over banks,
twenty feet above flood stage,
chased an invalid aunt onto kitchen
cabinets to await salvation
by the rescue squad.
A car tried to ford the bridge
on the south side of town, flushed
off, dangled down the steep bank,
its driver sacrificed to raging history.

A hundred-year flood,
the news service trumpeted.
Bridges impassable on three sides
of town, some relatives stranded
away from their motel. Others,
boat-less, could not navigate
the high ground home.

You loved to laugh, quipped
one-liners to share the mirth.
I imagined you, a broad smile washed
over your face, as you pondered
the timing, your exiting with a splash,
had you been able to hover over
the scene, view it with us. Instead,
you reclined, stone faced, engulfed
in your satin lined ark,
that night at the funeral home,
a night swallowed up in floods.

If I Go Suddenly

A humid summer morning, plodding
through a need-to walk,
I encountered other pilgrims chasing
health. One, a gray haired senior,
walk more like a shuffle, leaning
to it like a horseman into wind,
looked at risk of toppling
on the sidewalk, if not from heart
attack, then bulging stomach,
full of no discipline.

Audio apparatus wired
to waist and earphones cuffed
to feed his happy head with lifting
music or maybe inspired words,
his whole-face smile belied
the facts. High blood pressure
and arthritis could likely start
the list. Still, he *good-morning'ed*

me with gusto. I walked my round,
the image taking hold, and sang
my song against the worried air.
Back home, my mind embraced
this thought—*strolling a garden
of green trees and God's bright
flowers, tuned to joy, leaning
into the future, smiling
at the world; a cheerful
way to go.*

Wesley Sims has published one chapbook of poetry, *When Night Comes* (Finishing Line Press, 2013). His work has appeared or is forthcoming in *Connecticut Review, G. W. Review, South Carolina Review, Liquid Imagination, Pine Mountain Sand and Gravel, Praxis Magazine, The Avocet, Nature Writing, Plum Tree Tavern, Pangolin Review, Magnets and Ladders, Bewildering Stories, Breath & Shadow, Artemis Journal,* and others.

www.ingramcontent.com/pod-product-compliance
Lightning Source LLC
Chambersburg PA
CBHW032132050726
47590CB00008B/3053